Buddhism – The Ultimate Guide for Beginners

About this book

If you want to learn the ways of Buddhism then this book is a must read. If you intend to practice Buddhist principles then this book will provide a great platform for getting started. You will learn the fundamentals of Buddhism without the usual heaviness of other books bearing the same topic. You will also learn about spatial awareness and more importantly yourself.

I wish you all the best on your pathway towards Buddhism.

Table of Contents

Introduction

Chapter 1 - What is Buddhism?

Chapter 2 - Getting to Know Siddharta Gautama

Chapter 3 - The Four Noble Truths

Chapter 4 - The Eight-Fold Path

Chapter 5 - The Five Precepts

Chapter 6 - How to Become a Buddhist

Conclusion

Introduction

I want to thank you for downloading my book, *"Buddhism – the ultimate guide for beginners"*. This book contains all the information that you need to develop an understanding of what the Buddhism religion stands for, and how to find inner peace by practicing the religion yourself.

Whether you are a mere enthusiast or somebody who seriously lives by the ways of Buddhism, this book will definitely help you. By reading this comprehensive compendium, you will not only be well-versed in the philosophies and principles of Buddhism; you will also learn about its practical applications.

Chapter 1 - What is Buddhism?

Buddhism provides a path or way of living towards spiritual development that can ultimately lead to enlightenment and the realization of what's real and what's true. Meditation and other Buddhist practices are a way to change oneself to become in touch with characteristics like wisdom, kindness, and awareness. Buddhism has built a tradition of shared experiences which have accumulated and evolved over its thousands of years of existence. These experiences serve as a solid foundation for those who wish to fully understand the principles. Therefore, becoming a Buddhist or reaching the point of enlightenment is not an impossible task, especially if the one who seeks it are persevering and serious in intent. The ultimate goal of the Buddhist spiritual life is, in simple terms, to end all forms of suffering.

Buddhism is not about worshipping a God or a creator. Therefore in the "western sense" Buddhism is not at all a religion. The foundational tenets of the teachings of Buddhism can be described as direct and pragmatic: nothing lasts forever; all actions entail a certain result; and it is possible to attain change. Buddhism is somewhat universal – it can reach out and touch the concerns of all people despite their nationality, race, sexuality, social class, or gender. The methods that it teaches are very practical and they can be used to transform individuals into people who are capable of taking responsibility of the events that are occurring in their lives.

As it currently stands, there are approximately 350,000,000 people practicing Buddhism worldwide. Most of these people were initially from the East, but Asians and Westerners are slowly changing this. Buddhism is catching the attention of Westerners because of its practical nature. Buddhism can be practiced in different ways but the underlying principles are basically the same and involve eliminating a dogma, seeking a path of non-violence, having a conscious effort to tolerate difference, and practicing the methods of meditation.

Instead of a religion, Buddhism is referred to as a spiritual tradition. As a tradition, its focal point is on the development of the person and their spirituality. In their journey, they aspire to get to the state called "nirvana" which was first reached by the first Buddha, Siddharta Gautama. He successfully reached that point, otherwise known as the state of Enlightenment, during the sixth century before Christ.

Buddhists beliefs are centered on meditation, morality and wisdom, and they believe that it is possible to do that even without a God. They also believe in the three signs of existence, namely: uncertainty, suffering, and impermanence. Collectively, they are called the "tilakhana". Buddhism also supports the belief of endless existence, believing that everyone is reincarnated continuously. Reincarnation is the only way to fully understand the nature of suffering.

Nothing – be it good or bad – will last forever. The impermanent nature of things shows us that change is bound to happen. And it is our innate nature to combat these changes that results in sufferings.

Buddhism – Major Schools of Thought

To understand Buddhism, it is important to be well-versed in the different schools of thought. For beginners, it is important to be aware of the two biggest schools – one which is popular in Cambodia, Thailand, Sri Lanka, Myanmar (formerly Burma), and Laos which is called "Theravada" Buddhism. "Mahayana" Buddhism is the other prevailing Buddhist school of thought that is dominant in Mongolia, Korea, Japan, Taiwan, China, and Tibet.

A great majority of the Buddhist population do not have the intent to convert and preach. There are exceptions here, one of which is "Nichiren" Buddhism which is known for proselytizing.

Despite the minor differences that these major schools of thought bear, one thing is common: they all aid people who believe in the system of faith and who aspire to seek the path towards enlightenment.

Some Important Information

- ✓ There are at least 350,000,000 practicing Buddhism

- ✓ Buddhism rose to fame when Siddharta Gautama was able to successfully reach Nirvana in the sixth century before Christ.

- ✓ Buddhism is unique because it does not dwell on having a relationship with God. A personal God is definitely not a prerequisite.

- ✓ Worship can be done by Buddhists both in a temple and at home.

- ✓ The enlightenment path is possible to attain for those who seek it through constant development and practice of meditation, morality, and wisdom.

Chapter 2 - Getting to Know Siddharta Gautama

The first Buddha, Siddharta Gautama was a royal born in Nepal. His birth occurred some 2500 years ago. During the early parts of his life, he was used to all the luxury and privilege of living as a member of the royal class. One day when he decided to go out of the enclosure provided for the royal class, he met, for the first time in his life, an aged man, another who is sick, and a dead body. Because he was very disturbed by the experience, he decided to become a monk and he also thought that it should be right to adopt a vow of poverty – specifically the extreme poverty as illustrated by Indian asceticism. However, he was not completely satisfied by a lifestyle of poverty so he decided to craft his own path which he called the "Middle Path". This path is unique because it embraces neither luxury nor poverty.

One day, he was seated beside a tree associated to awakening, known as the Bodhi tree. According to the followers of Buddhism, aside this tree Siddharta was able to meditate deeply and was able to reflect about his life experiences. He decided from this time forward to be enlightened. By leading a life of enlightenment, he felt a lot of pain and suffering. Ultimately by following the enlightenment path, he was led to rebirth by virtue. During the famous meditation at the Bodhi tree, he meditated for 40 days and on a full moon that May, freedom was attained by Siddharta and he became Buddha.

Buddhism originates from Buddha. Buddha is an entitlement for those who are already awake. Siddharta was the first to be a Buddha, but he neither claimed to be a prophet nor a God. He was simply an "awakened human being" who had a deep understanding of life. If not for his meeting with the old man, the ill man, and the dead, he would have never realized the harsh realities of aging, sickness, and death. It was a puzzle for him because he had lived an overprotected and sheltered life. In his quest towards enlightenment, he became well-versed on the truth of life.

The Buddhists have a belief that when they reach the state of Enlightenment, they go beyond any worldly problems or trials.

Experiences in the normal world are all bound by conditions – the way we were raised, our mental and physical conditions, the way we see things, and people's points of view. When you are already enlightened, these conditions no longer matter. Enlightenment only brings out the deepest understanding of the most profound things in life – and suffering, though still existent, becomes more acceptable and manageable. Remember that it was suffering that pushed Siddharta to start his quest towards enlightenment in the first place.

In the last forty-five years of his life, the Buddha spent his time traveling, mostly in the northern part of India. During that time, he spread what he already knew to help those who were seeking enlightenment too. In the East, his teachings became known as the instructions towards enlightenment or the "Buddha Dharma".

Towards the end of his life, he made a significant difference by reaching out to people from different walks of live. He was able to gain many disciples and he led them towards enlightenment.

In turn, they went out to guide people and the Buddha Dharma became a chain that is difficult to break. The teachings were passed on and they were able to survive the odds even up to this day.

Siddharta made it clear that he was not claiming divinity at all. He put a lot of efforts to transform his mind and heart so that they could exceed the usual limitations. He affirmed that each individual can become a Buddha if enough effort is put in. Without a doubt, Siddharta was an ideal human being. He was, and he still is, a guide that can lead everyone towards one goal – the path towards enlightenment.

Chapter 3 - The Four Noble Truths

When Buddha was able to reach the point of enlightenment, he had a unique vision. He envisioned human beings, as a collective, as a bed of lotus flowers.

The lotus flowers come in different forms:

- Those that are still in the mud, submerged;
- Those who are just coming out of the mud; and
- Those who have reached the point of blooming.

Therefore, each person, in his own special time is bound to bloom and reach the point of enlightenment if he will be actively seeking it. Upon reaching that point himself, the Buddha decided to go on actively teaching and sharing what he learned throughout his journey. His goal was rather simple, to help people out in finding a way to grow towards the path of enlightenment.

As mentioned in the previous chapter, life seen through the lens of Buddhism is a life that embraces continuous and endless changes. The practice of Buddhism will help in taking advantage of this particular fact. Changing oneself, Buddhism recognizes, is not an easy task. But if the mind will be conditioned towards embracing change, it will be easier to manage the difficulties in life.

Most importantly, Buddhism advocates for the practice of meditation. This is one established way of developing a positive mindset. Also, you tend to manifest positive characteristics after doing so. Among the manifestations are the following: calmness, capability to sustain concentration, a heightened level of awareness and positive emotions towards other people. The awareness level attained from meditation makes it possible for anyone to get a fuller and better understanding of oneself. You tend to become a better comrade to people around you and you gain be deeper understanding about life in general.

Note that Buddhists never aim to evangelize per se. Neither do they aim to coerce others to believe in what they believe in. But it should be noted that they are very generous to those who seek knowledge from them, and they help people who are professing that they are actively searching for the path towards enlightenment. Also, they leave it to the individual to decide how much or how little of their advocacies they desire to apply in their own lives.

The most essential formulations of the teaching of Buddha are expressed by the Four Aryan or Noble Truths.

Aryan or Noble Truth #1: The Aryan or Noble Truth of the Dukkha as a component of conditioned existence

"Dukkha", a multi-faceted word, literally means anything that is not easy to bear or carry. It can stand for stress, suffering, anguish, pain, lack or absence of satisfaction, and affliction. The Dukkha is either subtly or grossly manifested. It can either be a mental of physical burden and pain or a torment that attacks one's inner being by presenting conflicts and other malaise that are existential by nature.

Aryan or Noble Truth #2: The Aryan or Noble Truth of the Dukkha that each suffering happens for a reason

The very cause is identified as the refusal to face change characterized by clinginess, aversion, and grasping on to the present reality. On one hand, this may be noted by one manipulating everything and anything and grabbing onto something or trying to pin that thing down. On the other hand, it could represent the pushing away of other possibilities. The process of identifying what we want permanently makes us differentiate what's "mine" and what's owned by people other than "me". Again, the three signs of existence are the following: the Annica (Impermanence), the Dukkha (Stress or Suffering), and the Anatta (No Self). Due to the fact that anything that exists with a condition is impermanent, such things will only lead to Dukkha. This also implies that there is no such thing as a permanent change. Reality, as we know it, therefore, is not permanent and is always changing. Therefore, there is no point clinging on to anything! By grasping onto any reality, we tend to push away all the others that this world has to offer. The attempts to manipulate the reality as we know it makes things limited for us.

Aryan or Noble Truth #3: The Aryan or Noble Truth that Dukkha will only end by achieving or reaching Nirvana

Once you get the hang of letting go of what's not permanent, you let go of conditional existence. This will allow you to progress to an unconditional existence that is frequently associated with the awakening and enlightenment. It is like waking up into a new notion of truth, a higher level of reality. It is awakening our Buddha nature. Some define the Nirvana as a boundless meaning, going beyond time and space. Therefore, Nirvana is a condition that goes beyond the borders of any definition.

In its literal sense, Nirvana actually means "not bounded". In one of the popular sayings, the mind was described as something that is similar to fire. It cannot be bound by any enclosure. But it should be clear that the analogy refers only to the flame, not the wick. The "flame" in the sense of the Nirvana keeps on burning even without the combustible material. It continues to glow and give out heat and light even without the wick. It cannot be extinguished. Nirvana is living a life giving out the light without getting consumed. When you are awakened, you have no fear of being extinguished because you will continuously give out light and glow regardless of not having a wick.

Aryan or Noble Truth #4: The Aryan or Noble Truth of the Path or the Way that leads to the State of Awakening

If you will look at it closely, the way or the path towards awakening is actually a paradox. It gives you the necessary conditions so that you can achieve an unconditioned living. If you are an outsider to Buddhism, this is difficult to reconcile. But one thing must be clear, awakening cannot be considered as a product of any factors that you stumble upon in your life. Even the Buddha's teachings cannot take you there. It is not "fabricated" by any methods. Instead, awakening should be regarded as something that you possess all along but you were unable to realize. It is a suppressed nature that has always been in our subconscious. But our nature to cling on to the limited, and our attempts to gain control of what cannot be controlled makes our "awakened" nature obscured if not totally abandoned.

Note that the path is a process that can help one move or remove beyond what's conditioned. In that context, the path is just about unlearning things. It is more of unlearning than learning – and that makes it more difficult to obtain.

The Buddha tells us that his teaching is like a raft. In order to successfully cross any river that is turbulent, you will need to build a raft. Upon crossing the river, the raft's purpose is over. You no longer need to bring it around with you. Therefore, in finding the path towards enlightenment, you need not cling onto anything – not even to the teachings of Buddhism. Once you find your way across, you should learn to let go. Everything handed over to you in this life are tools, and not dogmas. It is just like pointing your finger up to where the moon is. You should never get confused about which is the finger and which is the moon.

Chapter 4 - The Eight-Fold Path

The eight-fold path, otherwise known as Buddha's Noble Eightfold Path, is recognized to be one of Buddhism's most popular teachings. Its origins can be traced back to Siddharta Gautama's experiences, hence, it is one of the most ancient lessons that Buddhism can impart.

It can be traced back to Buddha's original conversations and therefore, it is highly valued and regarded as one of the treasured wisdoms of Buddhism. It is known for it practicality – it is very easy to apply its lesson is our daily lives. The teaching traditionally is perceived as the major "limbs" or eight areas of "proper" or "perfect" practice.

Path #1: Samma Dithi or the Perfect or Complete Vision

Otherwise translated as the right understanding or view, Samma Dithi refers to the vision or perception of the path of transformation and reality. There are two major classifications of the right view:

1. The Mundane View or the View with Taints: This type of view will only bring merit and give support to the favorable existence of the sentimental being within the samsara realm.

2. The Supermundane View or the View without Taints: This type of view is considered as a factor of the Way or the Path and it will only lead the holder to the liberation or self-awakening from the samsara realm.

The right perception comes with several aspects. Lay followers only sufficiently understand its simplest form. Other forms of this path require a higher level of understanding; therefore, only monastics are able to understand this. The following realities have to be fully understood:

> Karma, the Moral Law: All actions (be it by speech, thought, or action) will entail reactions (also known as karmic results). All actions, be it unwholesome or

wholesome, will results in a correspondent and proportionate effect to the original nature of the action. This is how all moral processes in our world should be viewed.

- The Three Traits: All the things that arise will die out and cease. Our body and mental phenomena will not last forever. And our tendency to cling on to this is the ultimate source of suffering.

- The Nature of Suffering: Aging, birth, death, sickness, sorrow, pain, lamentation, grief, despair, and distress are different forms of suffering. Our inability to achieve what we want is another form of suffering. Craving for something is the source of suffering; our ability to respond to that craving is the primary cause of the end of suffering. Ignorance, as a quality, is another probable cause of suffering. Education is also another approach to end all sufferings. The eightfold path is the most reliable way to bring cessation to all kinds of suffering.

Path #2: Samma Sankappa or the Path of Perfected Aspiration or Emotion

The second path, otherwise known as the right attitude or thought, requires the liberation of emotional intelligence within one's life. Another way to achieve this is through acting with sincerity, compassion, and love. People with a heart that is informed and a mind that can feel are most ready to practice the art of letting go.

Path #3: Samma Vaca or the Path of Whole or Perfected Speech

This is otherwise known as the right speech. In talking to others, we need to be not only truthful, but also clear, non-harmful, and uplifting. We should not hurt with our tongue.

The right speech is referred to as the capability to make use of the best words that will fit the intended message. Also, as much as possible, you should not tell any lies, or anything that can divide or hurt other people. In addition to that, people should not dwell on idle chatters. These are the conditions towards practicing the right or perfect speech.

False speech should also be abandoned. Only the truth should be firmly held and spoken throughout the world. Enlightenment is not for deceivers. According to the Tathagata, the following words are not spoken by a true Buddhist:

1. Words that are not factual, unbeneficial, untrue, disagreeable, and non-endearing;
2. Words that are factual but may bring about unbeneficial effects and might cause disagreement and can end any forms of endearment;
3. Words that are factual and beneficial but may bring about disagreement and end of endearment;
4. Words that are factual, at the same time, beneficial and agreeable, but can end endearment;
5. Words that are not factual, not true, not beneficial, but agreeable and endearing;

However, if the Tathagata knows that the words he heard are true, factual, agreeable, endearing, and beneficial; he has the right to determine the proper timing by which he will divulge what he knows. This is due to the fact that having sympathy for all beings is truly important and it should be one of the top considerations.

In any of the cases above, if the information is neither true nor beneficial nor is it timely, it should not be uttered. The Buddha was able to do this several times in his life. When he was asked about the nature of the universe and other things that are of metaphysical nature, he quickly dismissed the issue saying "it doesn't further". Therefore, our personal opportunities do not get furthered or benefitted by the knowledge about the fate of the universe; hence it might be best leaving that question unanswered.

Path #4: Samma Kammanta or the Path of Integral Action

This is otherwise known as the path of the right or proper action. This is considered as the ethical and philosophical foundation for life that is based on the non-exploitation principle of others and oneself.

This path is also translated into a more commonly understood terminology, correct and proper conduct. Therefore, the practitioner of Buddhism should be able to successfully train himself in maintaining uprightness in all his activities. He should not act in ways that are immoral and corrupt. In all of his actions, harming others or oneself should never be an option.

According to the Pali and Chinese Canon, the right action is avoiding, by all means, to take any form of life, avoiding stealing, and avoiding sexual misconduct.

On the other hand, Magga Vibhanga Sutta shares that the right action is not taking away one's life and veering away from unchastity.

Meanwhile, the popular Cunda Kammaraputta Sutta explains that the proper action is abandoning "killing" as an option, abstaining from taking any form of life, being compassionate and merciful to all living kinds who roam the earth. If it is not given to you, you should never take it. Misconduct in the sensual sense is also abandoned. People who are still in the protection of their fathers, mothers, sisters, brothers, other relatives, or Dhamma should not be involved in sexual acts. Also, women who have husbands or those who are already "crowned" by other men "with flowers" should not be subjects of sexual activities.

Path #5: Samma Ajiva or the Path of Proper Livelihood

Otherwise known as the path of proper livelihood, this is also founded on the principle of non-exploitation. This ethical law is also being used as the very foundational basis of an ideal society.

By all means, the following should not be the form of your business:

1. Selling Weapons: The act of trading any kind of weapons or instruments that can be used in killing should be avoided.

2. Selling Human Beings: The act of trading slaves, meddling with prostitution, selling or buying of adults and children are unforgiveable.

3. Selling Meat: Selling "meat" or dead bodies of (formerly) living beings after they were killed. Therefore, in a strict sense, breeding any kinds of animals and subjecting them to slaughtering afterwards is not acceptable.

4. Selling Intoxicants: The manufacture and selling or buying of drinks that are intoxicating and drugs that are addictive should not be allowed.

5. Selling Poison: The trade and production of poison or chemicals that are toxic or those that are formulated to kill should not be allowed.

Path #6: Samma Vayama or the Path of Energy, Vitality, and Fullest Effort

This is also known as diligence or right effort. This path involves the conscious directing of life energy to the way of transformation towards healing and creation of wholeness. This also involves the acts leading to conscious evolution.

The following are the four stages of diligence:

1. The act of prevention of unwholesomeness that does not originate from within oneself.

2. The act of letting go of the unwholesomeness that originated from within oneself.

3. The act of bringing up the wholesome acts that does not originate from within oneself.

4. The act of maintaining the wholesome acts that originated from within oneself.

Path #7: Samma Sati or the Path of Thorough or Complete Awareness

This is also referred to as the path of the proper mindfulness. In the process, you will develop awareness about yourself inside and out. The levels of awareness and the degree of mindfulness can be about oneself, the things around you and the thoughts and feelings of people around you.

Proper mindfulness can also be translated as the proper memory, the correct awareness, and the right attention. Practitioners are expected to be constantly alert for the possibility of occurrence of phenomena or events that will have direct effects on the mind and the body. Practitioners of Buddhism are expected to be deliberate and mindful, but they should also make sure that they never act out of forgetfulness or inattention.

What then can be considered as right mindfulness?

1. Making sure that the practitioner remains as focused as possible to the body and what happens to it – aware and ardent at all times. In addition, they should also be veering away from distress and greed at all times.

2. One should remain focused on the feeling towards and within oneself.

3. One should maintain a focused mind.

4. One should be aware of his personal mental qualities.

All of these can be practiced by anyone regardless of gender.

Path #8: Samma Samadhi or the Path of Full, Holistic, and Integral Samadhi

The eighth path actually refers to the capability to do meditation and concentration with the aim of absorbing what needs to be absorbed in order to gain a focused and one-pointed mind. Actually, these are mere attempts to translate what "Samma Samadhi" actually is. In the literal sense, "Samadhi" refers to the things that are fixed, established, and absorbed along a single point of focus. If the meaning is to be taken a notch higher, it goes on to represent a particular establishment, which can refer to but is not limited to the mind. Meaning it can also refer to the other parts of the entirety and it can explore other levels of awareness and consciousness. At this level, Buddhism is appreciated and understood.

According to Buddhists, the following refers to proper concentration:

1. Practitioners should neglect their own desires. Therefore, they should eliminate thoughts that are not wholesome. They should also abide to the first level of meditative absorption which goes with applied and sustained thought, bliss, and joy.

2. Abiding to the second level of meditative absorption that gives due focus to inner tranquility. Inner tranquility represents the unification of the mind.

3. Next, this can refer to the act of detaching oneself from his notion of joy in correspondence to mindfulness, equanimity, and understanding of his own bodily desires. This leads to the third level of meditative absorption.

4. Lastly, letting go of both suffering and bliss by allowing joy and sorrow to disappear. This is the fourth and final level of meditative absorption.

Chapter 5 - The Five Precepts

Buddhist teachings are preserved carefully and strictly by followers of Theravada Buddhism. Most of these are kept in the Pali language. One of the most popular teachings that all beginners in Buddhism should understand is the Five Precepts. The following are the five precepts, translated to English:

1. I make sure that I observe the precept of abstinence from destroying any form of life.

2. I make sure that I observe the precept of abstinence from taking something that is not given.

3. I make sure that I observe the precept of abstinence from all forms of sexual misconduct.

4. I make sure that I observe the precept of abstinence from lies and other forms of falsehood.

5. I make sure that I observe the precept of abstinence from all forms of intoxicants that may cloud my thinking and may lead to careless acts.

The five precepts may be considered as the Code of Morality and Proper Conduct of the practitioners of Buddhism. However, they should not be mistaken as commandments. Ideally, the precepts are carried out by virtue of free will. Nobody imposes these precepts into any of the followers.

However, you might be wondering if there are any practical applications of these precepts in our daily living. Are they still relevant today? If you ask any Buddhist, their response will be a simple "yes".

It is a way to train oneself to maintain uprightness in morals, in thought, and in action. It takes some conscious effort to develop these, but without a set of standards, training would be impossible. This is what the precepts are able to provide.

The five precepts may be summarized as ideals that produce desirable characteristics and qualities of the spirit. For example, the first of the five precepts aim to communicate kindness, compassion, and goodwill. Next, the second of the five precepts intend to communicate right livelihood, honesty, contentment, non-attachment, altruism, service, and generosity. And then, the third of the five precepts assist in the cultivation of qualities like sense of control of sexual desires, renunciation, mastery over senses and emotions, and self-restraint. The fourth of the five precepts leads to the path towards moral integrity, reliability, and honesty. Lastly, the fifth of the five precepts communicates the importance of wisdom, clarity of the mind, and proper mindfulness.

For those who are still in the process of familiarizing themselves with Buddhism, it might be a great idea to start with standards that are easy to follow. One by one, the desired characteristics will be developed. And little by little, the difficult task will be less and less daunting.

Chapter 6 - How to Become a Buddhist

If you are serious about leading a Buddhist way of life, and if you really wish to pursue the path of a Buddhist, the following are some guidelines that you should follow by heart:

- Question your motivation. Motivation is an important element of decision making. If you are moving from your current faith to Buddhism, this should somewhat be reflected upon if not scrutinized. What's your intention for abandoning your old system of faith? Are you motivated by the desire to achieve wisdom, mindfulness, and compassion? If so, congratulations. You are doing it for the right reasons. However, if you are merely driven by selfish desires like fame and pride, you should think again. The source of any practice is rooted to motivation. Therefore, if you want to be sincere in terms of practice, your motivation should also be sincerely wholesome.

- Commit first that you will practice Buddhism wholeheartedly. Manifestation of faith is actually a responsibility, so you should keep that in mind. Also, keeping a clean mind and heart for the effective practice of proper speech, appropriate thought, and wholesome action is not a joke. It requires a lot of effort. Remember if your sincerity and commitment are strong enough, you can be sure that you will reap better and sweeter fruits from your endeavor.

- By all means, the five precepts of Buddhism should be followed. Yes, it is not a mandatory Code of Conduct (as stated in the previous Chapter of this compendium). However, if you are serious about taking this path towards awakening, you should do every single effort to try. In any case, you should make sure that your mind and body are properly aligned to do this properly. Only then can your actions generate insight and proper wisdom.

- Check your lifestyle: it should be kept as simple and as healthy as possible. If simplicity and healthy living are your aim from the very beginning, then you won't have any problem. However, if you are coming from somewhere very luxurious, consider doing some adjustments even before you make that commitment to abide by the system of faith of Buddhism.

- Do prior research. If you have reached this point reading this compendium, you've gone a long way with your research already. But never limit yourself to a single material. You can also ask practitioners near you to enlighten you about the Buddhist practice. You will not only learn much about this; you will benefit much from the sharing.

- Consistently practice the prescribed path. This way, you will not only become a better believer but in the process, you will become a better human being.

- Find a good mentor within your community. This way, you will be properly guided. Chances are, you will have a better chance of reaching Nirvana. Proper guidance and instruction would play a big role in your practice as a Buddhist. Also, surrounding yourself with people who are into faithful and obedient practice will help you do the same.

➢ On a regular basis, you should give time studying the teachings of Buddha. This will deepen your level of understanding of the teachings. It will inform and inspire you at the same time towards proper and productive practice. Find peers who will help you study the teachings and deepen your faith.

➢ Keep an open heart and an open mind. Learning is a lifelong process and you should be open for all the opportunities that may come along the way. Never be discouraged if you find something you can't understand. Do not force yourself if you find anything difficult to comprehend. Be consistent and be confident. Your role is to sustain your efforts. It won't be easy but it will be worth it.

Keeping the moral high ground definitely is one of the biggest challenges any practitioner of Buddhism is faced with. Accept the changes that come your way and never cling onto the wrong things. After all, the act of clinging on will only bring you suffering. With an open mind and heart, you will be ready to receive the highest form of knowledge.

Best of luck with your quest towards awakening and enlightenment.

]

Conclusion

Thank you again for downloading this book!

This book has provided you with the information required for an aspiring Buddhist. This system of faith is not only interesting; it also presents principles that are worth living.

The next step is to understand and reflect on the things about the Buddhist faith that were presented in this book. Best of luck!

Finally, if you found this book helpful, please take the time to share your thoughts and post a review on Amazon. It'd be greatly appreciated!

Printed in Great Britain
by Amazon.co.uk, Ltd.,
Marston Gate.